Amazon.com

First published by Amazon/CreateSpace

ISBN-13: 978-1484958056

ISBN-10: 1484958055

Printed in the United States of America

This book is printed on acid-free and recycled products.

Writing

as Readers Want It!

By

Darrell Berkheimer

Amazon/CreateSpace

Dedication

This book is the result of many years of writing passion.

It is dedicated to:

- My dear friend and companion, Rita Matheson;

- Carmen Winslow, Managing Editor at *The Montana Standard*, for her assistance in reporting on my various retirement projects;

- Warner B. Bair II of Deer Lodge, Montana, for his friendship;

- The guest speakers and students who attended my communications and writing classes, sponsored by the Butte School District's Adult Community Education program.

Contents

Foreword

This is a book for both beginning writers and authors wondering why their stories and manuscripts have not been selling.

It's also for all others who must prepare articles, proposals and reports for their work.

It emphasizes the most basic principle in marketing – that people won't buy whatever you're selling unless it's attractive to them! That remains true whether you're selling a story, a project proposal, an idea, or yourself.

Unfortunately, much of the writing produced today often fails to meet that attractiveness objective. The writing simply is not keeping pace with the times.

Attention historians, professors, biographers and many other non-fiction writers: You're continuing to produce wordy 19th century writing in the 21st century.

The writing produced by academic writers is among the worst, according to Thomas Sowell, economist and conservative political philosopher.

Sowell noted in an essay on writing that he at one time served as an editor – editing academic writers. He referred to it as "the most painful kind of editing." He added:

"Too many academics write as if plain English is beneath their dignity, and some seem to regard logic as an unconstitutional infringement of their freedom of speech. Others love to document the obvious and arbitrarily assume what is crucial."

With comments like that, this book should be considered crucial for all academic writers.

It is designed especially to help beginning writers polish their writing. And it will note how to begin the often agonizing effort of getting published.

We live in a fast-paced world. And reading – in contrast – is a slow-paced activity.

As a result, writers, editors and publishers must improve the ease of reading if they intend to remain competitive with the many technological distractions and gadgets that appear so much more inviting.

And writers in business must display writing skills that assist in drawing business from competitors.

It is the reader's **right** to expect quick comprehension, or to be entertained. And it is a writer's **obligation** to meet such standards.

So this book concentrates on the mechanics of writing and the need to use various techniques and devices – to make reading easier, more interesting and influence others.

The principles of this book are formulated to meet the desires of the greatest living authority on writing – the readers!

All of the principles listed are designed to give the readers what they want and deserve!

And if you apply these principles, readers will like you, and they will believe you. They will understand you, and they will stay with you.

That is the reader response that you must get! Otherwise, readers will ignore you and your writing effort will have been wasted!

Those italicized words paraphrase wording in the Foreword of the best little book on public speaking ever published. It's titled *"Public Speaking as Listeners Like It."*

That book is cited because many of the principles in it apply to writers and readers just as they apply to speakers and listeners.

And that book prompted the title for this book.

That little book on public speaking was written by Richard C. Borden and published in 1935. The book is out of print, but copies are being sought – because it continues to be cited in classes on public speaking.

It's a hardbound book that measures only 5 inches wide by 7½ inches high. It is quite thin with only 111 pages. It has narrow columns, 12-point type with extra spacing between lines, and lots of white space.

Borden's book demonstrates that the size of the book is not what makes it great – but how well it fulfills its objective!

That excellent little book has considerably less than 20,000 words in it.

Publishers today should be ashamed when they instruct an author to expand a manuscript to 120,000 words or more – especially when it was an excellent product with 75,000 words or less.

How many times have you, as a reader, skipped over long, wordy descriptions so you could get back to the action, or the information, that you sought?

And how many times have you heard others repeat that same remark?

Good writing should not be padded.

Good writing uses fewer words rather than more.

Good writing is crisp, clear and concise.

Good writing uses only the minimum words necessary to convey the desired information or picturesque vision.

This book concentrates on those principles as it cites helpful tips and examples to improve writing and publication chances.

All types of writing are considered – not just fiction and books.

The tips and techniques noted will improve writing for magazines, newspapers and newsletters, reports and proposals for business, writing to persuade, humor and speech writing.

Examples will be provided throughout the book – concluding with a series of writing and speech checklists, after several previously published letters to the editor and editorials.

New writers also will see how much easier it is to become published today. But just being published does not mean their books will be purchased and read.

Promotion and marketing can be just as difficult and costly as ever, with success sometimes requiring as much luck as winning a lottery.

And the low pay that comes with many writing fields also will be noted.

1 – Demand for Better Writing!

Why do we write?

We write for various reasons. We write to inform, to entertain, to make people think, to initiate action, and to fulfill work assignments.

But most of all we write because we expect others to read what we have written.

So the importance of good writing cannot be over-emphasized – because people just don't like to read poor writing.

It's a practical issue. What is not well written is not well read. And in business, good writing provides credibility to the source of the writing.

Executives throughout business and government will tell you that writing is one of the most important skills an ambitious young person can have. The person who is able to write simply and clearly – in addition to having technical knowledge and experience – is more likely to get the job of his or her choice, and to succeed quickly in that position.

People who do not like to write – or are reluctant to do so for whatever reason – often attempt to get by with talk instead. Sometimes that works – for a while. But oral communication can cause problems and waste time, money and energy – when the writing of a detailed note or memo would provide the clarity that's needed.

A friend once asked: "What do you expect to accomplish with your writing?"

It caught me a bit by surprise; so I thought for a few moments before answering.

Then I replied that if I simply make people think about various issues – and what might be done to make changes for the better – then I have accomplished something rather important.

I explained the role of writers is to present the information, raise the important questions, and identify alternatives and possibilities. Writers generally don't have any better answers than their readers.

Good writers realize readers not only want to know what and who, but – even more importantly – they want to know why. They want to know the effects of various events and issues.

Readers want to know how problems can be solved. And businesses, industries and governments want well-written information on how projects can be accomplished as quickly and cheaply as possible.

All organizations and supervisors want

specific details and costs; but they don't want to struggle through a lot of wasted words.

Other readers just want to be led into a fantasy world where they can relax and escape from the various demands and pressures in their lives. And they have a right to expect good writing to provide that escape – without an abundance of description and wordiness.

So all writing must be geared to the intended audience. But the best writing always establishes an informal, friendly tone for readers. Even business writing is best when it's pleasant to read, rather than too formal and impersonal.

The use of first person – such as "we and I" – is much more comfortable to business readers than statements quoting "the company" and referring to the "undersigned."

Increasing Emphasis on Writing

As our nation evolved from a Manufacturing-Industrial Society to an Information and Services Society, writing skills became more in demand.

In manufacturing, oral communications were important – to explain to workers what they needed to accomplish. But communications then were not nearly as important as they are today in our Information Society – and in today's global competition.

In international operations, most jobs involve exchanges of ideas and concepts that require vastly more precise communications. Writing – with clarity – provides the preciseness that is demanded.

And writing helps eliminate problems with people in different countries using different languages.

In business, the role of writing is to provide a communication that is available when, or until, it is needed.

Some writers, however, apparently use writing to impress, rather than to explain, persuade or entertain. Instead, we must use writing simply to perform a service.

Writers make their best impression with readers when their objective is simply to communicate and inform as quickly and succinctly as possible.

2 – A Bookstore Visit!

(The passion in this essay is what prompted this book.)

As I was paying my bill at the bookstore, I told the clerk: "No wonder book sales are declining; so many of the books are written so poorly."

"I agree," she said.

I went to the store to purchase a couple of good biographies. But much of the writing in the books I examined contained many long sentences and large blocks of drab-looking black print. I didn't want to subject myself to struggling with that type of reading.

That visit prompted me to think about which types of writing and books continue to sell well, while many others continue to decline.

Sales of books, magazines and newspapers have been declining for many years – in comparison to population growth. That's nothing new. And it's obvious that many electronic distractions are the reasons.

The decline began in earnest with the expansion of television to round-the-clock programming. But the greatest decline came as a result of the Internet and the many electronic gadgets equipped with computer chips -- including video games.

Meanwhile, printed matter has failed to improve substantially to compete with all the distractions.

The books that continue to sell well are the fast-paced novels with lots of dialogue by engaging characters. They offer short paragraphs and lots of eye-relief white space. Other writings continue to lose sales as people turn to the Internet, the gadgets and the games.

In today's market, simply writing about interesting and informative subjects is not enough. Today's writers also must improve their packaging. They must provide fast-paced comprehension with writing that's easy to read.

My latest bookstore visit revealed a multitude of poor writing that has failed to change with our times. The worst writing examples are non-fiction writers in general, academics and historians in particular.

Much of the non-fiction that I examined was foreboding, intimidating and wordy.

Would-be readers are turned off by paragraphs that go on for 15, 30, and 50 or more lines. I don't want to deal with the struggle of reading paragraphs that begin on one page and end one or two pages later.

Writing like that is slow reading – requiring

deeper concentration, and too much of the reader's time.

Two books on the life of Harry Truman looked inviting. And I was drawn to another about Theodore Roosevelt. But after examining the pages upon pages of gray dreariness inside, I put them back on the shelf.

I opted instead for two books that appeared to be better written and easier to read – about James Garner and Carol Burnett. The book on Garner's life was touted as a primer on ethics. And Burnett's book was promoted as one of "laughter and reflection."

Most of today's books are packaged well on the outside – with interesting excerpts and comments on stylish covers. But many of the interiors are drab. The books simply lack crisp writing and needed eye relief.

Simple and concise writing is needed to draw today's readers. Writers must shorten their sentences to simple, declarative statements. Rarely should a sentence have more than one dependent clause.

In addition, most paragraphs should be limited to two and three sentences. I told my writing students that they have a better chance of seeing the sun rise in the west than seeing one of my paragraphs with four long sentences.

Newspaper editors are well aware of the need for shorter paragraphs and sentences because of the narrow columns. They also are well aware of the need for simplicity and fast-paced reporting to retain readers.

Newspapers editors also have learned to use boldface subheads to vary the dreary, gray type. Authors and other editors would be wise to do the same.

And long paragraphs that contain a series of items or thoughts should be reworked into lists – lists that provide a separate line for each item or thought. Those lists can be numbered, or further accentuated with a dash, small black square, or dot at the beginning of each item.

A switch to a different type font, italics or boldface will draw attention to the list – or some other feature that might deserve emphasis. Even type in color could be used to provide variety from all the gray and black.

Activities in today's world are fast-paced. Reading is one of the slower-paced activities. And when the writing sets a pace that's too slow, or appears too bland, it won't be read.

So writers and publishers need to employ every device they can to maintain and build readership.

In that vein, writers would be wise to keep chapters short – as another device to improve reading. Readers do not like to be stuck in the middle of long chapters when they must turn to other demands on their time.

But to maintain interest, writers might consider adding a short one- or two-sentence promotion at the end of each chapter about the material in the next chapter. Such promos work well on the front pages of newspapers. They send you to stories on the inside pages.

I believe a substantial number of readers in younger generations will continue to prefer some paper books to electronic copies only. Electronic copies simply aren't as convenient as a hard copy when you want to find something that you underlined or highlighted.

And few people will want to loan their Kindle, Nook or Kobo the way they can loan the hard copy of a book.

So I submit that those paper books that meet the criteria set by younger generations will be better written and easier to read than many in the bookstores today.

3 – Beginning Needs Pizazz!

Readers won't do it!

Readers just won't stay with you if you can't write a beginning that attracts and holds their attention.

And that flame of interest should be ignited with the very first paragraph – with the first few sentences.

Why waste your time and effort if you can't develop a good beginning?

The "quick, hard punch" that I just used is one method. It's a good one that provides excellent results.

Picture your potential readers – holding what you have written in their hands – as they think about the many other activities they should or could be doing.

Will your beginning hold them? Or will they decide that doing something else is more interesting or important?

Louis L'Amour was one writer whose beginnings offer excellent examples of how to draw in the reader. He wrote more than 100 novels; and several hundred million copies were sold.

One reason for his success was his ability to grab and hold the reader's attention from the very beginning. He often did it with dialogue in the first paragraph.

The beginning – whether in writing or public speaking – should be one or two crisp sentences that make immediate sense.

Here are some examples that I used at the beginning of several articles in my first book – *Stories from The Golden Throne.* Three of the four were used to begin weekly columns published by the newspapers where I worked.

■ *"Generally, banana cream pies are among my favorite pastries. But not the one I had on Saturday night."*

■ *"His death came a month shy of his 15th birthday. That was less than three weeks ago, and the lingering feelings now are of guilt rather than grieving."*

■ *"Some people might have referred to him as a bum, or a drunk – as some of his actions and statements indicated. But he deserved no less respect than any other person; so I listened."*

■ *"Grand Teton National Park has provided me with an attitude adjustment!"*

Each example raises questions designed to draw the reader into more reading to learn the answers. Readers want to learn the answers to why – or how.

Too often, beginning writers tend to get involved in "setting the stage" rather than jumping into the meat of the story, or the conclusion of the report.

Many folks learned – back in high school – that writers need to provide answers to the all-important questions of *who, what, where, when and why.* In addition, journalism instructors might add *how, and how much.*

But all of those questions do not need to be answered immediately.

Good beginnings start with a bang instead of a whimper. Reader interest can be captured quickly by a startling or unexpected beginning about a subject or incident.

An unknown writer faces stricter parameters than a known author who already has best sellers on the market.

Many unknown writers will go unnoticed simply because they fail to begin with one of three techniques -- dialogue, immediate action, or by creating a question that triggers the reader's desire to know more. And one of the three had better come during the first page.

Only established, well-known authors can ignore those three techniques.

Readers browsing in a bookstore will check the comments on the front and rear covers of a book. Then they might leaf through it, checking how the book is written, and perhaps the chapter titles and first page.

That first page by a writer unknown to the reader better have an enticing beginning, or the unknown author can miss an important sales opportunity.

Writing for Business

Of course, when preparing a report or project proposal for your business or employer, you need to begin with "the bottom line," then report reasons or facts to substantiate your conclusions.

But the recipient of your writing still will expect brevity in presenting those details.

Conscientious writers will rewrite and revise their beginning numerous times before they settle on something that satisfies them.

Even daily media writers, facing a deadline in a half-hour, may spend the first five minutes or more of that valuable time on just the beginning.

Beginnings sometimes come easier when writers develop the habit of either drafting a short overview or selecting one major aspect that can be reported in just one or two sentences.

If it helps to begin with stage-setting in the first draft of your manuscript or proposal, then do so. But when you begin to edit and rewrite, skip down a few paragraphs to something with more "meat" in it to use for your beginning.

As a newspaper reporter, I covered many council, board and commission meetings. And those groups often discussed and acted on numerous agenda items. So I usually selected one or two items that appeared the most important to emphasize in a short first paragraph.

Then I might begin the second paragraph in this manner:

"In other action, council adopted a revised animal control ordinance, allocated funds to purchase a new ambulance, and discussed city hall maintenance issues."

Readers deserve to know quickly about all issues included in a news story or business report. After that, the writer can go into detail on those items – one at a time.

Suppose council acted on a total of nine items. After a short one- or two-paragraph beginning, I might list each one with a separate short line or paragraph after a dash or bullet. Again, then I would follow with details on each, one at a time.

On some occasions, when city council took action on several items of relatively equal importance, I might begin this way:

"County commissioners took four major actions this morning."

Then I might list the four quickly in the second paragraph.

Proposal Writing

Suppose your company is one of several invited to submit a construction proposal. And in preparing for it, you developed three alternatives. Which one should you submit?

Or perhaps you want to list all three, but can't decide which to list first – especially if you have no idea how much money is available for the project. Then, maybe the best way to begin is:

"Our company can offer three alternative plans for this project – ranging in cost from $1.7 million to $2.4 million."

It does not matter how interesting, entertaining, or how much money you might save with your project, if you cannot spawn interest in the first few sentences, you may have wasted your opportunity. That's the bottom line.

A community development consultant, instructing a class on writing project proposals, raised this issue:

If your proposal is one of two receiving equal consideration by an agency, that agency will be looking for a reason to reject one of the two. Would you want the plan you submitted to be rejected simply because it was deemed to be poorly written?

Expertise in writing is an indication of expertise in other work.

4 – The Best Writing!

So after you have captured your reader's attention with a good beginning, then what?

You must retain interest with an easy and natural flow. And the best flow for writing is a conversational style – as if you are sitting across the table from someone and telling the information.

But writing should flow even better than conversation. That usually means plenty of time spent on rewriting and editing.

Novelist and screenwriter Elmore Leonard wrote: "If it sounds like writing, I rewrite it." He also advises: "Try to leave out the part that readers tend to skip."

What tends to impress readers the most – perhaps even without them realizing it – is the ease of reading that results from brevity, simplicity and good organization.

Writing coaches and editors find it impossible to over-emphasize those attributes.

Conclusions: The best writing offers quick comprehension. And readers like a fast-paced delivery.

Many fiction authors and their editors are

aware of this. They strive for fast-paced action with engaging characters. That's why fiction books continue to sell well.

The book **The Elements of Style**, by William Strunk and E.B. White, states:

"*Vigorous writing is concise. A sentence should contain no unnecessary words, a paragraph no unnecessary sentences, for the same reason that a drawing should contain no unnecessary lines and a machine no unnecessary parts. This requires not that a writer make all his sentences short, or that he avoid all detail and treat his subject only in outline, but that every word tell.*"

For Quick Comprehension

One study revealed readers have 100 percent comprehension of a 12-word sentence. That compares with 85 percent from a 17-word sentence – and a decline to only 10 percent comprehension from a 43-word sentence.

Long paragraphs also make reading more difficult and reduce comprehension.

Long sentences should be examined to determine if they should be separated into two sentences. Or maybe two sentences would be better as three shorter ones.

Remember: Ease of reading with a natural flow is the objective. If you can't read it out loud to yourself with an easy flow, it needs to be reworked.

And don't hesitate to begin a sentence with a conjunction such as *and, but* or *so*.

Yes, I know that English teachers and grammarians for many years have advised against doing that. But if using a conjunction to start a sentence – or even a paragraph – serves to provide easier reading with shorter sentences, then do it!

We begin with conjunctions frequently in our speech. And, after all, who are you writing for? English teachers – or readers?

Occasional use of the unconventional sometimes can be quite effective.

Need for Eye Relief

Long, compound-complex sentences, and long paragraphs that create large blocks of black or gray type, are intimidating to the reader's eyes. They make reading more difficult and reduce understanding.

Shorter sentences and paragraphs, instead, tend to create feelings of immediacy, intimacy and drama.

Yet many people – including some professional writers and many non-fiction authors – apparently have failed to realize the importance of frequent paragraphing.

Today's readers have many desires and demands tugging at them for their time. And reader studies have concluded the easier – and more interesting – we make it for readers to devour our writing, the more our writing will be devoured.

Large blocks of type and long sentences cause readers to lose their place when interrupted. But shorter paragraphs of one to three sentences make it easy for them to return to where they were.

That's because the white space between paragraphs provides needed eye relief.

Shorter paragraphs become even more important when publishing restrictions do not allow for a full line of space between paragraphs – which is most desirable for ease of reading.

Without that line of space, the partially empty lines at the end of paragraphs, and the indentations at the beginning of the next paragraphs can provide eye relief.

Some publications – to make it easier on the reader – will provide an extra half-line of space between paragraphs.

Reader eye relief is just as important in writing as comic relief is necessary in good dramas. Both are needed to break mounting tension. For readers, it's mounting eye tension. And anything that makes it easier for readers makes writing more attractive.

Dialogue provides ease of reading. A major reason is the frequent paragraphing that results in switching from one speaker to another.

Poetry is another example. It's easy to read for the same reason – lots of white space.

Variety, however, remains the spice of life. So readers will accept the occasional long paragraph and long sentence. But in general, sentences should be limited to only one dependent clause. And paragraphs of more than four short sentences should be extremely rare.

In varying the length of paragraphs, a short declarative sentence – standing alone – can provide considerable emphasis to that statement.

Boldface category headings – such as the one above – also provide white space and ease of reading.

5 – Vocabulary & Phraseology!

Good writers search for words that provide the "exact shade of meaning" they want.

It is that search – to express the proper tone, and most delicate of nuances – that provides "distinction and individuality" to writing.

Dale Carnegie, in his best-selling books on how to influence people, wrote:

"Many people blunder through a long lifetime – after leaving school – without any conscious effort to enrich their use of words.

"They use the overworked and exhausted phrases of the office and the street. Small wonder their talk lacks distinction and individuality."

It should be obvious that good writers will always have a dictionary and thesaurus within arm's reach of their word processor.

Suppose you have written that a character was *surprised*. But then you decided that surprised just does not capture the nuance or feeling you wanted to convey. So you decide to check the thesaurus to find a more suitable word or better phrasing for your purpose.

The thesaurus provided this list: *shocked, startled, stunned, astonished, perplexed, puzzled, confounded, stymied, mystified, bewildered, unexpected,* and *unsuspected.*

Now you can select the one with the most appropriate meaning!

*"**The Word** -- An Associated Press Guide to Good News Writing,"* states:

"Writing is the art of the second thought. What first springs to mind is seldom good enough; the skill lies not in a ready gush of words, but in sifting them. Sometimes that process is swift, sometimes it takes longer ... Attention to detail is at the heart of good writing."

Later, the same book adds: Tone "is primarily generated by the choice of words." And a writer should "select details that the reader can see."

Best-selling novelists are good at using words and phrases to create a mind-picture that the reader visualizes.

Richard Borden, in his book on public speaking, writes that listeners want phraseology that is pleasing. He adds:

"It means that your choice of words must reflect listeners' preference for the specific, the colorful, the picturesque."

Borden's advice applies just as emphatically to writing.

I recall during my college days when one instructor talked in terms of the "common cents" value of words. He advocated the use of "quarter words."

He explained the majority of people talk and write with "nickel and dime words," rather than the quarter words that are more precise, yet familiar to everyone.

He also advised that we should avoid using the "big words" – "the half-dollar and dollar words."

He labeled "half-dollar and dollar words" as pompous and flowery.

He advised that we learn those words, then forget about using them – because it is only important that we know them.

Writing with pompous words merely indicates pompous writers.

Use of technical terms also should be taboo unless you are sure all your readers will know their meanings. Technical terms should be relegated to the publications for whatever particular profession is involved.

Readers not only prefer, but demand, that writers use familiar words.

But beware of using trite clichés, frequently used colloquialisms, slang and gutter talk. Use such verbiage rarely. Occasionally such words are appropriate; but really good writing will limit their uses to a bare minimum. Then they have more effect!

Good writers also refrain from using words that are absolute or extreme, such as "always and never." Those words are exaggerations that have become shopworn, threadbare and trite.

They are exaggerations that are over-used in speech. They usually are not appropriate because true life – realism – is a tale of exceptions.

Instead of always, consider using words such as often or frequently. Instead of never, consider using seldom or rarely. A second choice might be the use of qualifiers such as "nearly" always or "almost" never.

Two other words that should nearly always be deleted are "very" and "really." Rarely will they add anything.

Good writers also must be conscious of using favorite words too often. That's another occasion to be reaching for the thesaurus.

Search for words that are more specific. Have the courage to be distinctive. Strive to create your own similes, metaphors and analogies.

Adding up and down, out and over after so many verbs can destroy the punch of good writing. Broadcasters especially are guilty of fostering such misuse.

For instance: Is something coming any faster if we say "coming up next" rather than just "coming next?"

Why write "close up" or "shut down?" Are they closed or shut any tighter by adding up or down?

When we "tighten up" or "tie down" something, is it any tighter than when we just tighten or tie it?

Can't we just use clean, clear, slow or pour rather than clean up, clear up, slow down or pour out?

Instead of "giving up," can't we be more specific with such words as relinquish, surrender or sacrifice?

Why should we destroy the beauty, the dynamics and specificity of our language?

A good rule for better writing is: If you hear it often from broadcasters and in street talk, then you probably can find more appropriate wording by reaching for the thesaurus.

Finally, I saved this next issue for last – because I want it to linger in your mind after reading this chapter.

Readers get quite angry when they must search for the meaning of initials.

For some reason, many writers today either have forgotten or decided to ignore the old rule of putting the initials in parentheses immediately behind the first use of a long title or organization's name.

Then, several paragraphs later, when that title or organization is referred to only by its initials, readers must search for the first use of the complete name or title – because so many such initials simply are not that well known.

And if the title or organization is cited again many paragraphs or pages later, the full title or name should be repeated – again with the initials immediately following in parentheses.

Why anger readers unnecessarily by failing to be a little considerate?

Readers want to know each word symbolized by each letter in an acronym – and they don't like searching to learn them.

6 – Passion & Purpose!

Readers are drawn to words that contain passion in them.

And that passion is seldom in the words unless that passion existed in the writer.

The most successful writers have a passion for writing that almost becomes an obsession.

The need for passion in writing was quite well explained more than 120 years ago in a guidebook for newspaper writers. It was published in 1890 by the *New York Sun.* That guidebook stated:

"You don't find feelings in written words unless there were feelings in the person who used them. With all their apparent independence, they (words) seem to be little vessels that hold in some puzzling fashion exactly what was put into them.

"You can put tears into them, as though they were so many little buckets; and you can hang smiles along them, like Monday's clothes line, or you can starch them with facts and stand them up like a picket fence; but you won't get the tears out unless you first put them in.

"... It isn't the way the words are strung together that makes Lincoln's Gettysburg Address immortal, but the feelings that were in the man. But how do such little, plain words manage to keep their grip on such feelings? That is the miracle."

This book cites various tips and techniques to attract and retain readers, yet I am willing to admit that a number of them can be ignored if the passion in the writing is strong enough!

Warner B. Bair II, a mystery-thriller author in Deer Lodge, Montana, explained he writes with a certain compulsion that stems from the continuing development of his characters.

He reported the main characters in his novels "live" within his mind. As he goes about his various activities, he envisions situations and events that spawn his desire to put his characters in those settings.

Because he has developed his characters so vividly in his mind, he foresees how his characters would react to various situations and stimuli. He feels a compulsion – a passion – to write about what his characters would do.

He has written a series of novels with those same characters. And as he moves from one novel to the next, he sees his characters growing and developing more intricately as a result of their previous experiences in his stories.

Bair employs a somewhat unusual twist for his main character, who he never refers to by a given name. So his books with the anonymous character are referred to as the "Anon Series."

That creates some writing difficulties for Bair – when he needs to have other characters hailing his anonymous man.

The Role of Purpose

Bair also reported that his ravenous reading revealed to him that it is the characters that drive the plot rather than the reverse. He noted it is character development that makes the plot work.

Perhaps it is that same compulsion that Bair describes about himself that prompts so many best-selling authors to become so prolific in the numbers of novels they produce.

Many successful authors apparently have that compelling need to express and explain, inform or entertain. It's a compelling need to get their thoughts and ideas into print.

That is their purpose. That is my purpose.

And it can provide the biggest satisfaction

that is available in life – offering others what we have to give.

A few writers have been able to get away with extensive "stage setting" – because of the acclaim they have received for what comes after. One such writer is James Michener.

In many of his books, Michener starts with the beginning of time and creation as the reader struggles through the first 50 or 60 pages. But readers continue through that struggle because they have learned that the narrative takes a turn to excellence for the remainder of the 400 to 700 pages of his books.

Readers know that Michener's fiction is based on historical events, and that his fictional characters are well developed toward providing a great understanding of that history. That obviously is the purpose of his writing.

I'm not sure how many readers are aware of the points and purpose of the westerns written by Louis L'Amour – because so many of them appear to be written simply for fast reading and entertainment.

L'Amour has written that his novels are geographically and historically correct, with little deviation. But his novels also are quite philosophical – with emphasis on ethics, morality and chivalry.

In a speech presented at a Toastmasters meeting, I referred to L'Amour as my "Mystery Philosopher." That speech later became a newspaper column published shortly after his death when I was City Editor at *The Daily Times* at Farmington, N.M.

I believe L'Amour's purpose went well beyond writing books to entertain and make money. I believe his purpose included stating philosophical truisms and emphasizing the morality and ethics that should guide how we live our lives.

Beginning writers seem to have difficulty limiting themselves to the purpose or general theme of their story. They allow themselves to get sidetracked on unrelated events, issues or details, which become major distractions.

I also believe that if a writer's sole purpose is to make money, he or she is not likely to succeed. Without some degree of passion and compulsion, the writing will be bland. And bland writing fails to attract and hold the numbers of readers necessary to become an author of distinction.

Business writers also need some degree of passion and belief in their writing, or it will be bland and fail to produce the desired result.

It is that very blandness and lack of relevancy that has resulted in declines in circulation and sales for many magazines and newspapers. That was the topic of my commentary printed by *Editor & Publisher*, the news media's monthly trade publication.

That commentary – titled ***The Future of Newspapers?*** – is reprinted here:

What is the future of newspapers? Will they continue to shrink in existence as the growth of Internet reading continues? Can newspapers garner enough revenue from Internet readers to remain viable?

For more than 30 years, newspaper readership has been declining – particularly in relationship to population growth. There are many reasons – according to various studies and opinions. But I believe there is one reason that is more responsible than any other.

Newspaper readership has declined simply because newspapers have lost relevancy. They fail to provide pertinence to the lives of most readers.

Many daily newspapers continue today only because they offer the same old, dull news that is pertinent mostly to those people who grew up in the community and never left, and those who left briefly for education and then returned.

That's the news of births, obituaries, engagements and weddings, building permits, and the court dockets. Only a few feature stories and the sports section show some degree of passion for what's happening locally.

But communities have changed drastically with the mobility of our nation's population. Increasingly larger segments of today's communities are people who were raised in other cities and other states. The old standard news items have less significance to residents who came from elsewhere.

A century ago, newspapers showed real passion, but they lacked objectivity. They also lacked the problems resulting from the multitude of competitors provided by so many other news sources available today.

That passion of newspapers a century ago was most evident in political issues, but it also was evident through pride in public service and involvement in the controversial issues of the day.

The journalism of the mid-1900s, however, slowly shifted to objectivity over all else.

That statement should not be mistaken to indicate that objectivity is no longer important. It remains just as important as ever in everyday reporting.

But too many of today's newspapers are filled with an excess of news that is available from the multitude of other sources. And too little of today's papers is assigned to the passion involved in discovering, reporting, and interpreting the issues that affect local citizens.

Today's newspapers often allow only one full page daily for opinions and interpretations of the many controversial issues facing readers. And many of those pages contain opinion reports on national and world issues so readily available from other sources – and on issues which most local readers feel they can have little or no effect.

The management at so many newspapers appears afraid to take positions – apparently concerned that they might irritate readers. So what! That's what is needed!

Newspapers need to stir the pot. And they will even gain the respect of those who often disagree with the paper's positions. There is little relevancy for readers when newspapers continue to feed them pabulum.

Instead, newspapers need to open their pages to more opinions by surveying and soliciting comments by local readers. Readers need to feel that they are part of their local newspaper, and that their attitudes and opinions matter.

Local newspapers should be conducting surveys on what local citizens consider the most important local issues, and how they should be approached. Reporters should be interviewing the citizens who live in a different neighborhood each evening and reporting what they have to say.

Newspapers should be doing whatever it takes to identify the local problems most on the minds of local citizens, and to daily provide interpretive analyses and opinion pieces about those problems – properly labeled as opinions.

Newspapers must get out of the habit of limiting so much of their reporting to the so-called "experts" or "appropriate sources." Citizens are tired of hearing so much from those considered "leaders" in the community. They want to see – in print – what their neighbors and their friends across town have to say. They want to know how other communities have resolved similar local problems.

How can readers expect to show loyalty to the newspaper if the newspaper can't show more loyalty to what's relevant to the readers? It's time for newspapers to bring back more passion to the issues of their readers. They must find or develop ways to extract the passion of their readers and report that passion.

Simply put, today's newspapers are too bland. And only when they can overcome that blandness will they become relevant again.

# # #

Obviously, *Editor & Publisher* considered these passion issues worthy of bringing them to the attention of all its media readers.

41

7 – Interviewing & Writing!

Interviewing and writing is an art. It's the art of mixing credibility with sensitivity.

News people sometimes can be very demanding – even obnoxious.

I admit I was guilty of that on occasion during my newspaper career.

Balancing sensitivity with credibility can be extremely difficult for an interviewing writer.

Most media representatives realize the importance of being sensitive to the position and feelings of the one being interviewed. Yet the writer is expected to ask the difficult – often embarrassing and prying – questions that need to be asked to maintain credibility.

Readers and listeners can have mixed emotions. Their attitudes toward an interviewer may vary according to how much the reader or listener likes the person being interviewed.

It's an issue that fiction writers seldom face – unless they are the ones being interviewed. But it is one that news writers and researchers face frequently.

Interviewers strive to walk a fine line. They want the cooperation of the interviewee, yet know they need to ask those tough questions.

Most people want an interviewer to be aggressive at getting answers. Readers and listeners want straight answers. They want the truth.

The situation reminds me of an old black and white movie titled *The Night of the Hunter*, which starred Robert Mitchum. He was a serial killer who played a demented preacher.

He had H-A-T-E burned on the knuckles of one hand and L-O-V-E on the knuckles of the other. He would explain how the two struggled with one another as he clasped his hands together, with fingers intertwined, and rocked them back and forth.

That's how sensitivity and credibility battled one another in the newsrooms where I worked.

Readers do not want a Casper Milktoast-type news media that submits to the pressures of local officials, businesses and celebrities. People not only want to know what happened, but how and why.

And they also expect magazine and book writers to dig and get such information for them.

But sources and interviewees want sensitivity to their "special circumstances," and they can threaten to end an interview if they feel sensitivity is lacking.

So the situation can require considerable tact by the interviewer.

Barbara Walters used a phraseology that worked well in allowing her to tactfully ask difficult questions. She would say: "My listeners will never forgive me if I fail to ask this question: ..."

When sources are uncooperative, the public deserves appropriate commentary. The public needs to be reminded that truth and appropriate details may not be available because the source refused to disclose such information.

Writers owe it to their readers to report when they believe sources are hiding such information and details. Readers don't like superficial portrayals.

8 – Cautionary Advice!

Low pay for writers, the need for confirmation and skepticism, and discretion in the use of quotes are several areas deserving cautionary advice.

For non-fiction and business writers – especially media journalists – I advise a generous dose of caution on the use of quotes. We have all heard these complaints:

- **"I was misquoted."**
- **"I didn't say it that way."**
- **"It was taken out of context."**

Unfortunately, too often those complaints are valid – all because a poorly trained writer failed to use discretion.

News media writers, particularly, seem to think they need to use colorful quotes in order to have a good story. And seldom do print and broadcast editors give good instructions on how and when to use quotes.

They should be advised to use caution and be discerning.

The idea that frequent quotes are needed throughout a report usually is wrong. What is more important is concise paraphrasing that quickly conveys the proper meaning and the points that the information source was trying to make.

There are only ▄ four reasons for using a quote. The first two apply to most occasions, while the last two are limited to special circumstances. They are:

- *When the quote states something so well that it can't be stated any better or more concise;*

- *When the quote provides a certain accurate and needed flavor or color to the story – which otherwise would be missing if it was not used.*

- *To highlight exchanges and testimony in trials, hearings, meetings and other garrulous encounters.*

- *For pertinence. Newsworthy speeches require considerable direct quotation. It's advisable to give significant passages in the speaker's own words, even if they lack sparkle.*

Other than those reasons, it is more important to accurately report how issues were emphasized rather than searching for "good quotes" that can be demeaning to the source.

Many journalists, including some of the best writers and broadcasters, can't speak nearly as well as they can write. That's simply because writing provides more opportunity to think about grammar and which wording is best.

Because few of us are capable of always speaking with excellent diction, we might use double negatives or poor sentence construction. We might even make some silly statement that seems almost opposite to the point we are trying to make.

That particular statement – by itself – when quoted out of context, can make us sound ridiculous or nonsensical.

Common Sense and Respect

Poorly trained writers might seek out such glitches and highlight them in their reports. Is it any wonder we hear complaints such as the ones noted above?

Responsible writers concentrate on the objectives, issues and tone of the speaker. And when possible, they will repeat to the source their understanding of what was said to confirm the meaning.

When writers no longer are guilty of making slips of the tongue when speaking, only then will they have a right to be insensitive to the slips of others.

Brevity – a sensible report on the issues emphasized by the source – should be the writer's main objective.

Selecting quotes merely to be sensational, misleading or demeaning is unethical and irresponsible. Instead, common sense and respect should prevail.

Common sense and discretion also are needed in the use of profanity and slang.

Despite these precautions, quotes remain important. They provide authenticity and sparkle to writing.

The Association Press book, **The Word**, observes that the art in the use of quotes "comes down to knowing when to quote, when to paraphrase, and when to forget the whole thing."

The Need for Confirmation

Good editors and business executives do not like single-source articles or reports when controversial issues are involved.

They want additional sources to confirm conclusions in controversial issues. And they usually expect to see contradictory views from other sources. Then the reporting is more objective rather than subjective.

Failure to seek contradictory views opens the door to criticisms of a slanted or one-sided report.

Single-source items should be reserved for "personality spotlights" – designed to feature the views and activities of a single person, and often presented with the question-and-answer format.

Beware of presenting conclusions as facts. Conclusions resulting from studies and research usually are open to various interpretations and subject to further study.

Skepticism Is Healthy

Most of us have a tendency to be too accepting of what we heard or saw. That's when a healthy dose of skepticism becomes important. That skepticism is important especially when we hear rumors.

The best print and broadcast media managers are diligent about training reporters to be skeptics – to guard against immediate acceptance and judgment of what they read or heard.

Good media managers issue strong warnings against repeating unconfirmed or unjustified statements – especially because of the potential legal ramifications.

And skepticism is important particularly when an expert or authority in one field is commenting on another area not related to his or her area of expertise.

The thinking and questioning – which comes from reading different views – also can yield a skepticism that helps us pause before jumping to errant conclusions.

Unfortunately, our public education system and religious organizations spend too much time teaching us to memorize and blindly follow rather than to THINK and QUESTION.

Reading different authors exposes us to a variety of opinions – sometimes contradictory – which foster questioning and critical thinking. It's the habit of critical thinking – resulting from skepticism – that helps us make decisions when information appears contradictory.

A related admonition, often repeated by good editors, is: "Never assume; never, never assume."

Many writers and reporters found themselves in difficult situations – sometimes serious legal problems – as a result of an assumption. That's why it is so important to confirm what you heard or thought you saw.

And few writers are paid enough to deal with legal problems – especially if they must do so on their own, without the backing of an employer.

Writers Poorly Paid

Many talented writers and authors will never earn high incomes. That's partly because of the competition in those fields and partly because of the undervalue attached to many writing occupations.

That's unfortunate – because many writers have well-developed analytical skills as a result of their reading, research and work experiences.

The public has attached a certain glamour to writers and media workers. I suspect that has the effect of drawing an abundance of people into those fields. And whenever supply outstrips demand, it usually results in a low-fee, low-pay situation.

A recent Forbes article on the "Most Surprising Low-Paying Jobs" included radio and television announcers and reporters and correspondents.

The article reported the big pay for those positions is offered in only the top media markets such as the Washington, DC, New York and Boston areas.

This bleak picture may appear contradictory to statements in chapter one that noted an increasing emphasis on writing.

In chapter one, it is noted that "executives throughout business and government will tell you that writing is one of the most important skills an ambitious young person can have."

The next statement adds that a "person who is able to write simply and clearly – **in addition to having technical knowledge and experience** – is more likely to get the job of his or her choice, and to succeed quickly in that position."

That statement explains that good writers are in demand when they have expertise in other fields – and not just in media work alone.

But it also indicates that good writing is in demand throughout all the other professions.

9 – Getting Published!

Getting published is seldom easy – unless you pay for it yourself.

That's true even when you have written a story that is better than many of the others you have seen published.

But you can take steps to improve your chances. And more alternatives are available today – at less cost – than in years past.

The steps begin with a profuse amount of reading, and an abundance of writing. Seek and study the books that are well written, and read many in the genre you wish to write.

Novelist Barbara Kingsolver wrote:

"I learned to write by reading the kind of books I wished I'd written."

How you write usually results from what you read. So if you want to write well, you should read good writing. And good writing is best when it is fun to read.

When the subject of writing is raised, many people think only in terms of writing a book – a novel. But getting short stories and magazine articles published should be the first goal.

Many novels – perhaps most – resulted from expanded short stories.

That requires a bit of research – to identify the periodicals most likely to publish the type of story or article that you've written.

Expect rejections, however. They are the dues most writers have paid long before the arrival of sweet success.

Naturally, rejections hurt. They gnaw away at your confidence. So intermediary steps should be considered – to boost your ego and rebuild your confidence.

Consider writing letters to the editor of newspapers or magazines – on timely subjects.

Hey!... it's a way of getting published. It's a start. It's a way of re-booting your confidence.

If a letter is short, well written on a timely subject, the chances of it being published are quite good. The subject should be one on which you have a strong opinion; and don't neglect to do any necessary research.

For tips on techniques and examples of previously published letters to the editor, turn to the chapter on Writing to Influence, Page 69.

Also: Newspaper and magazine editors often are willing to publish personality spotlight stories as a result of one-on-one interviews with a local celebrity. And consider getting one or two photos to submit with any magazine article.

It should be obvious that you need to examine various publications and how the articles are written and presented in them – before you submit any.

And if you have not already developed a working knowledge of grammar and punctuation, then you will need to have your writing edited by someone who has. It's always wise to have someone else read and edit your work, regardless of how skilled you might be.

When you have attained the first goal of getting published in periodicals, be sure to examine the changes that were made to your writing in the published version.

I repeat: Be sure to examine the changes that were made to your writing. That is a most important learning process.

When you complete a manuscript for that first book, you have more publication choices today than ever before. But chances of getting a big cash advance from a traditional publisher are less than ever before.

The days of six-figure book advances for unknown writers have disappeared. Even five-figure advances are unlikely for a previously unpublished author.

The publishing world has changed considerably in recent years. The many large publishing houses of years past have dwindled to fewer than a half-dozen mega-publishers with many subsidiaries referred to as imprints. Those imprints tend to concentrate or certain types of books or niches.

Few writers are aware of the many imprints and their niches. That's a major reason for obtaining an agent.

In addition, small regional publishers operate by selecting manuscripts on subjects mainly of interest to their regions.

Writers may have better luck by contacting such publishers if their manuscripts are geographically oriented.

Chances of success are slim if you choose to submit your manuscript randomly. Those chances will improve considerably if you can interest a good agent to represent you. That likely will require some research.

And beware of any agents who want payment up front for anything more than copying and mailing your manuscript. That could be like throwing money down the toilet.

It can take weeks or months to find a good agent, and years can be spent seeking a publisher – without any success.

Fortunately, other publication choices have developed and improved in recent years. But they nearly always require dipping into your bank accounts.

The other options are self-publishing, subsidy publishing, and e-publishing.

Self-publishing can be relatively cheap if you have the abilities to prepare and design every part of the book so that it is "camera-ready" for printing.

In a few weeks, it is possible to have the first 50 copies of a 180-page book printed and sent to you for less than $180!

But that is only if you have the editing and rewriting skills, can design your own front and rear covers, and can format the interior pages properly.

Then the big questions are: How do you promote and market it?

Promoting and marketing can be quite expensive – and produce small results.

Self-publishing also has a somewhat disreputable image. It is the residue of contempt the industry has had for "vanity" publishing – when presses will publish virtually anything an author is willing to pay them to print.

As a result, authors who have used the vanity presses tend to be shunned by the more legitimate publishers and authors.

Subsidy publishing has developed as a result of the demand for an alternative between the vanity presses and rejections by traditional publishers.

In subsidy publishing, the author can choose whether to perform a necessary task or pay to have it done. But always have someone else edit the manuscript.

In addition, the better subsidy publishers will require the author to meet certain standards before agreeing to publish the book.

Subsidy publishing also is much faster than traditional publishing. It may take only a few months compared to the year or more that's usually involved in traditional publishing.

Many of the problems of publishing are detailed by Warner B. Bair II, a mystery-thriller author in Deer Lodge, Montana. Bair is an excellent writer of thrillers who has experienced many of those difficulties. In his blog – http://warnerbbairii.com – he wrote:

"The biggest problem with subsidy publishing is the stigma that is still attached to having your book published in this manner. Although the

major book chains will carry a subsidy-published book on their web sites, they will absolutely not stock your book on their shelves. They have exclusive agreements with the major trade publishers and will only stock a major trade published book."

"Another problem is cost. On a cafeteria plan, you can end up spending thousands of dollars publishing and promoting your book through a subsidy publisher. A trade publisher, of course, pays for whatever these costs may be, costs for publishing and promotion."

E-publishing is another possibility. It involves little or no cost if you can follow the formatting procedures. It also produces small returns in royalties and suffers from the same problems of self-publishing and subsidy-publishing – the stigma and a lack of promotion.

Both self-publishing and e-publishing are like buying a lottery ticket. You can't win if you don't buy a ticket, but the chances of winning are microscopically slim.

Such are the chances of having your book become a best seller.

10 – Humor & Speech Writing!

Og Mandino, in his book ***The Greatest Salesman in the World***, states: "I will laugh and my life will be lengthened for this is the great secret of long life ..."

I definitely agree with that statement!

It is humor that breaks tension between individuals.

It is humor that maintains interest in a subject.

It is humor that puts sparkle in a speech.

How do we become humorous? How do we develop humor in ourselves – in our speech and our writing?

Writers might try, but books and essays just can't tell us how to be humorous.

They can cite examples and tell us where we can find humor. Bill Cosby has shown us that one of the best places is in the imagination of our youth.

Books can provide us with thousands of examples – even hundreds of thousands. But humor is something we must develop on our own. It comes as part of our attitudes and outlook on life.

One of the best items of advice on developing humor comes from the book titled *The Public Speaker's Treasure Chest* by Herbert V. Prochnow and Herbert V. Prochnow Jr.

That book notes that many pertinent stories can be found throughout literature; and the Prochnows strongly recommend reading biographies.

Their book says: "Interesting facts and interesting incidents from interesting lives" can make the difference between the dull or worthwhile and the colorful essay or speech. "Searching until one finds this material pays rich rewards."

Authors advising on the use of humor usually will issue a strong warning that the <u>humor must be related to the topic</u>.

A touch of humor that brings only a smile, but is inherent to the topic, will outshine any loud guffaws resulting from something unrelated to the topic.

Obviously smooth transitions are impossible when the humor is unrelated.

And a desire for loud laughter is a common mistake made by many!

Often, the best humor – in writing or speech – is the recounting of an incident or situation that actually happened in the life of the writer or speaker. It comes more naturally – especially in speaking – because it is something that already is a part of memory.

Delivery, however, is most important. And delivery usually is easier when the humorous incident comes from our own experiences.

In that respect, the writer has the advantage of revising and rewriting. The speaker, however, must practice delivery to get the best results. Laughs usually depend more on the telling than the plot of a story.

But avoid using puns.

Richard C. Borden, in his book *Public Speaking as Listeners Like It!*, advises that a pun rarely gets the laugh that is expected. He says the pun carries with it "an unpleasant connotation of wise-cracking" that people dislike.

Borden and the Prochnows agree that listeners prefer humor in story form.

Humor and various stories to accentuate your writing and speech are available from many sources.

The Prochnows book is one of two that I bought for that purpose. The other is: *5000 One and Two Liners for Any and Every Occasion,* by Leopold Fechtner.

But, as already noted, the best humor usually comes from incidents in our own lives.

Listeners and readers particularly enjoy our humor when we are willing to laugh at ourselves. Many of us tend to be guilty of taking ourselves too seriously. So recounting those incidents when we goofed usually will bring the smiles and chuckles that we desire.

For more than 11 years, I worked with a woman who provided me with a great deal of laughter and daily smiles. Her name is Phyllis Phillips. For many years, she wrote most of the obituaries that appeared in *The Daily Herald* at Provo, Utah.

And the ability to write obituaries almost every day, week after week, definitely requires a sense of humor.

If we had to interrupt her during that duty, her frequent comment was, "Don't bother me; I'm obitching."

And when office bantering occasionally was directed her way, one of her standard comebacks was, "Bite the wall."

It was Phyllis who provided us with *"The Happy Birthday Dirge,"* which we started singing when birthdays of newsroom staff members were announced.

And then it became a dubious "honor" for the employees in other departments – when two or three of us were beckoned from the news staff to sing the dirge on their birthdays.

The event brought smiles and chuckles to all involved.

Here are the lyrics of its two stanzas, which must be sung with a quavering voice:

> *Oh Happy Birthday; Oh Happy Birthday.*
> *People dying everywhere;*
> *Gloom and misery in the air;*
> *But Happy Birthday; Oh Happy Birthday.*
> *One step closer to the grave;*
> *Think of all the food we'll save;*
> *But Happy Birthday; Oh Happy Birthday.*

(Phyllis noted her one daughter discovered the dirge, but had no idea of its author.)

I left that Utah newspaper in 1983 to become a managing editor in Georgia. But those of us who worked there will never forget the laughter and fun we shared as a result of the dirge provided by Phyllis.

For me, that fun has continued yearly as I have shared the dirge with many others where I have lived and worked since then.

When in Georgia I met Mike Owen, then a sports editor who was burned out on writing sports. So I assigned him to the news editor's position, but asked him to continue writing a weekly column on any subject of his choosing.

Mike applied a good sense of humor to his writing – similar in style to his favorite humorist, Lewis Grizzard.

I told Mike one day that I was leaving the office for a speaking engagement. I noted I would be explaining newspaper operations at a meeting of retired civil service employees. When I added I would probably only be gone about 45 minutes to an hour, he disagreed with me.

"I expect you'll be gone much longer than that," he said, pointing out that he knew I would be speaking to a large group.

"No, Mike, I'm not a long speaker," I said. I added that I usually only speak for about five to 10 minutes, and then ask for any questions from the audience.

"Oh, you'll be gone longer than that – you'll see," he argued.

When I returned in slightly less than an hour, he remarked:

"I am surprised. I would have bet you would be gone longer."

"I told you so," I said as I walked over next to him as he was working at his computer.

"I did just what I told you I would. I talked for no more than 10 minutes and then asked for questions."

Then I decided to tell a little joke on myself, as I leaned over Mike and added: "But I told them everything I know."

Mike got a smirk on his face, as he looked up from his computer and said in a slow, quiet voice:

"You must have told them twice!"

The bantering that occurs in offices and among family members are other good sources of humor. Often, it is the bantering between characters in novels and dramas that provides the comic relief.

And tales of our absent-minded actions work exceptionally well.

I recall when the company that processes debit cards for my bank committed a major blunder, which affected me and several other customers, including one of the bank's employees.

The company failed to mail out new debit cards before the old ones expired.

It was rather embarrassing that Saturday when the grocery store clerk reported payment was denied because my debit card had expired.

On Monday an express delivery to my bank was arranged for the new card. The bank called me when it arrived on Wednesday.

So for several days I knew that my old card was useless.

But on the drive to the bank to get my new card, I tried to buy gas with the old card!

Duh!

And I remember one day when I was news editor at a daily newspaper. I was advised at noon-time to tell the staff the computer system was off line and would not be available for a couple hours because of maintenance programming.

"Okay, I'll warn the staff," I replied. So I went to my desk, sat down and attempted to write a note in the computer telling the staff the computer was down.

Then I looked around sheepishly to see if anyone realized what I was trying to do!

Patrick F. McManus, a northern Idaho outdoor writer, is one of my favorite humorists. His short stories are interesting and easy to read – except for his frequent long paragraphs when he's not writing dialogue.

His humor columns, many of which appeared in outdoor magazines, were turned into at least a dozen books. In many of his stories, he refers to incidents in his youth in much the same vein as Garrison Keillor and Bill Cosby.

11 – Writing to Influence!

We can make a difference in our world when we can persuade and influence others. We all have that opportunity – because writing provides that opportunity.

All of us participate in persuasion when we attempt to sell our ideas and opinions to others.

And for those who have difficulty getting started on writing – or getting published – start with a subject on which you have strong opinions and feelings. Simply write what you think and go from there. Then edit, rewrite and polish it.

But to be successful at influencing and persuading others, we must impress one very important concept permanently in our minds. And that concept is:

Other people do things for their reasons ... not because I want them to!

That is the most important concept explained in Dale Carnegie's book – *How to Win Friends and Influence People.*

During my 28-year newspaper career, I wrote many columns and editorials designed to sway opinion, stir action and laud the good examples set by others.

The greatest rewards were the praising comments I received from readers.

In addition, my newspaper editorials won awards in both Utah and Texas.

Much of that came as a result of reading Carnegie's book. And many times I repeated his advice on why others do what they do.

When we keep in mind that other folks do things for their reasons, not ours, we can persuade and influence – because we gear our efforts toward their desires.

To act on that concept, we must consider the reasons that prompt others to act, and then emphasize those issues in what we write – using logic and reasoning.

As always, the beginning is the most important. It not only must draw the reader's interest, but it should personalize the issue by quickly pointing out how the reader is affected.

A good beginning can shock the reader with an unexpected statement.

Raising questions is another good way to draw in the reader. But questions must be worded to stir the reader's desire to know the answers. Or the questions should be phrased to draw the reader's immediate agreement.

A third good beginning will praise someone or an organization. Readers like to read praise. It provides a feel-good reaction. And from praise it can be easy to switch to a single, related issue that needs the reader's attention.

I can think of no better shock examples than two cited by Richard C. Borden in his book *Public Speaking as Listeners Like It!*

He cites a speech against profanity by clergyman Henry Ward Beecher, who began by stating: *"It's a God-damned hot day,"* which shocked his listeners. Then he added: *"That's what I heard a man say here this afternoon."*

Beecher subsequently proceeded to condemn such profanity.

In another example on how to begin a speech on traffic safety, Borden's suggested beginning is: *"Four hundred and fifty shiny new coffins were delivered to this city last Thursday."*

What better way could pique the interest of the listeners?

In a letter to the editor, I used this beginning:

All of the wrangling over wolves in our U.S. Rocky Mountains has become disgusting.

Both the shiny new coffins and wolves statements raise issues intended to draw readers into wanting to learn why.

The next example is the beginning of an editorial written when I was serving as managing editor of a newspaper in Texas. I wrote:

"We believe the Texas Supreme Court made a mistake this fall when it ruled that bar owners can be held legally liable in traffic deaths caused by drunken drivers who earlier had been patrons at the bar.
"What a ludicrous decision."

Again, readers want to know why the newspaper considers the ruling ludicrous.

Another letter to the editor used this beginning:

"The road crews in Montana and its counties deserve praise for the good work they do in snow removal each year along the state's major highways. But one failure presents a danger that could result in serious injuries and one or more deaths."

That beginning sings praises but prompts readers to learn about the failure.

Yet another example raises questions phrased so that readers agree with certain conclusions. That letter to the editor began this way:

"Have you noticed all of the expensive television advertising against a federal government-sponsored health-care system?

"Who do you think is providing the money to pay for all that expensive advertising?

"Doesn't it appear obvious that much of that money is being provided by the insurance and medical industries?"

The remainder of those letters will be provided at the end of this chapter – to answer the questions that they raise.

In various ways, each will exhibit one or more of six traits that should be considered and included in any writing to persuade and influence. They are:

1. **Concentrate on a single issue!**
2. **Present the case in a friendly way.**
   A compliment or praise works well.
3. **Appeal to noble motives.**
   Use wording that draws "yes, yes" responses.
4. **Show respect for the views of others.**
   Anticipate the thoughts and desires of your audience.
5. **Give facts; cite sources, and dramatize ideas.**
   Cite advantages and disadvantages rather than right or wrong.
6. **Sometimes it's best to simply throw out a challenge.**

We must be sure, however, that what we present as facts actually are facts – and not simply opinions or conclusions.

Studies and research usually provide conclusions that remain open to different interpretations and subject to further research. Be sure to emphasize those sources and situations.

Historical statistics, however, usually are facts that remain irrefutable.

We can sway readers and listeners more easily when we dramatize our ideas with examples. We must cite situations that readers and listeners can identify with – such as the many similar experiences we all had when we were young.

Sometimes we can reap the appropriate action or conclusion by appealing to a pride in honesty and fair play – by appealing to such noble motives. And a challenge can initiate a sense of competition that spawns a desire for improvement and change.

Should you choose to write letters to the editor, they should be kept short – no more than one page. And concentrating on a single issue helps to keep them short.

Complete Examples

What follows are several complete letters to the editor and two editorials. They display one or more of the six traits listed above. All were previously published.

Concerning wolves: Let the pros do their job

(Published as a Letter to the Editor)

All of the wrangling over wolves in our U.S. Rocky Mountains has become disgusting.

It's time for the bleeding hearts, hunters, livestock owners and politicians to tackle other, more important, issues that face this nation – and allow the wildlife management professionals to do their job.

Wildlife management professionals have been doing a good job throughout our United States. Because of them we usually have appropriate numbers of any game animals or fish that you want to mention – in accordance with the habitat available for each.

Why should there be any exception for wolves?

In many – perhaps most – cases, wildlife management professionals have initiated actions and restrictions that provide for the numbers of our wildlife and fish populations to increase – so that appropriate numbers can be harvested by hunters and anglers.

Our wildlife officials have initiated appropriate actions to control those populations so that we do not have exorbitant slaughters or over-harvesting, and so that we do not have an excessive road kill, winter deaths from starvation, or large kills as a result of pollution.

And the professionals have worked toward reducing pollution and increasing habitat where possible.

I won't say that they haven't made mistakes in judgment on occasion – because they have. But they are in a position to correct those mistakes by revising restrictions, permits and limits in the very next year or two.

Regarding wolves, I have not heard anyone who actually advocates eradication or elimination of wolves to extinction. Hunters and livestock owners as well as the other pressure groups have all indicated a desire to have wild populations of wolves in our wilderness areas for our children, grandchildren and other generations to come.

But we must remember that wolves, just like other large predators such as bears and cougars, have no natural enemies to cull their numbers – to keep them from becoming too abundant for their habitat. Man is their only natural predator. So harvesting by hunters and livestock owners, when their numbers become too large, is a natural controlling process.

Professionals are well equipped through various laws that give them the authority to set permits, limits and restrictions to control other wildlife populations. So now it is time to give them the authority to do the same with wolves – and for pressure groups to direct their attention to more important issues such as our economy and the failings of Congress.

The wolves letter begins with a hard-punching single sentence, but proceeds with a rational attitude that praises the work of wildlife officials. It dramatizes the issue and appeals to the noble motive of fairness for all.

# # #

Dangers at Interstate Ramps

(Published as a Letter to the Editor)

The road crews in Montana and its counties deserve praise for the good work they do in snow removal each year along the state's major highways. But one failure presents a danger that could result in serious injuries and one or more deaths.

I believe Montana has a nationwide reputation for doing a good job in snow removal – especially when people consider how often it snows in Montana.

When I was driving a tractor-trailer rig coast-to-coast, I never worried about traveling over Montana's passes. For example, Montana always had its portion of Lookout Pass well sanded.

But for the past several years, I noticed that Montana often fails to carry that good work over to the exit and entrance ramps.

With the interstate roads relatively clear – especially in the right lanes – many drivers in Montana will continue to travel at or near the 65 and

75 mph speed limits. But if they fail to slow down more than usual when approaching an exit ramp, they could be in serious trouble.

Another danger exists at the entrance ramps, which are designed for drivers to accelerate their vehicles so they can safely merge at interstate speeds when they reach the end of the ramp. That can be quite impossible when the entrance ramp has not been cleared of ice and snow.

If deaths occur, or some motorists are maimed as a result of the state's failure to clear the ramps – the state could face some major adverse reactions – perhaps even lawsuits.

For safety's sake – and to eliminate or reduce such potential problems – Montana needs to do a better job at those expressway ramps.

# # #

That example cites a single-issue failure after praising overall work in general. It dramatizes the issue by citing potential negative results if positive action is not taken.

The next letter ends with a question designed to have most people agreeing and saying yes. It concentrates on a single issue that affects all who purchase auto insurance. Limiting to a single issue helps to keep editorial essays short, providing more punch.

Motorcycle Helmets Issue

(Published as a Letter to the Editor)

I have noticed that Montana's helmet law for motorcycle riders is applicable only to riders who are 17 and under. That concerns me!

Years ago, I was against motorcycle helmet laws. Back then I considered it was just their tough luck if motorcycle riders turned themselves into a vegetable because they were too macho to wear a helmet.

But that was before I realized that my insurance premiums – and the premiums paid by all others – can and do increase when motorcycle riders maim themselves.

Accident statistics affect the actuarial tables used by all insurance companies. Even those accidents by motorcyclists covered by other insurance companies can affect the premiums that we must pay.

That means the hospital and treatment costs paid by any insurance company as a result of motorcycle accidents will affect the rates paid by everybody.

The bottom line is: I do not want to pay more for my insurance because some motorcyclists are too macho to wear helmets.

I believe motorcyclists should be required to pay more for their insurance if they don't want to wear helmets.

So my question to everyone else is: Do you want to pay more because they aren't required to wear helmets?

#

This next example continues with the series of questions noted in the beginning above. As the reader supplies the answers, the author expects to lead the reader to agreeing with the conclusion.

Health Care Waste

(Published as a Letter to the Editor)

Have you noticed all of the expensive television advertising against a federal government-sponsored health-care system?

Who do you think is providing the money to pay for all that expensive advertising?

Doesn't it appear obvious that much of that money is being provided by the insurance and medical industries?

After all, who stands to lose the most from a government operated health-care program?

Do you really think the average family or worker stands to lose the most? Or do you think the ones who stand to lose the most are the big profit-taking insurance and medical providers?

And who do you think provides the money for all those drug and insurance ads that appear on TV day and night all year long? Don't those ads cost many millions of dollars?

That's money that originally came from you and me when we paid for insurance and drugs!

And doesn't President Barack Obama raise a very telling issue when he talks about open-market advocates who claim that open competition always provides the best services and prices?

Then President Obama asks: If open competition always provides the best services at the best prices, what do the big health-care industries have to fear from a government-provided option?

I have no problem deciding what the answers are to these questions. That's why I want our Congress to enact a government-sponsored health-care option!

# # #

This next letter does not specifically tell whether the writer is for or against legalized abortions, but it cites the ramifications of banning abortions.

Abortion foes must realize ramifications

(Published as a Letter to the Editor)

Once again, we see a substantial segment of our society pushing to make abortions illegal. But seldom does anyone emphasize the ramifications of such actions.

Yes, we can cite those rare occasions when a premature fetus is taken from the mother months early and, against all odds, survives to become a healthy young child. But that is a very rare exception to reality.

And our doctors warn that more than 90 percent of such cases end in death, disfigurement and other cruel disabilities and complications -- resulting in enormous costs to the family, and a drain on the resources of our government and charitable services.

If we make most abortions illegal, then we must be willing to participate in helping our government and charitable agencies pay those tremendous costs.

But those pushing to make abortions illegal don't want to talk about that. Instead, they want to either eliminate or cut the very social services that are needed to deal with those children born with so many defects.

We can't have it both ways!

If we choose to support actions that eliminate or reduce abortions, then we must also choose to vote for the taxes that will be needed to finance the social services required to serve the children and families involved.

Even when such children are born healthy, many are born to unwed girls who usually are incapable of supporting themselves - without the addition of a child. Again, our social services are drained to help such individuals.

Many of us do not want the Social Security and Medicare services, which we paid into for so many years, to be reduced to assist those who likely will be unable to contribute anything to our society for much or all of their lives.

The anti-abortion folks do not want to talk about such ramifications. But more of us must be willing to emphasize the services that will be needed and the costs involved.

We must be willing to vote to pay the additional taxes needed to provide those services if we act to take away the mother's choice.

Are you willing to do that?

# # #

Drinking ruling was a mistake

(Originally published in *The Big Spring Herald*, Texas)

We believe the Texas Supreme Court made a mistake when it ruled that bar owners can be held legally liable in traffic deaths caused by drunken drivers who earlier had been patrons at the bar.

What a ludicrous decision.

We can only hope that the Supreme Court justices were half asleep, distracted or otherwise had an off day when they issued that ruling.

Whatever happened to that universal principle of accepting responsibility for our own actions – the one our parents strived so hard to teach to us.

It makes us think of when we were back in elementary school, when we tried to find others to blame for our actions. You remember – when you told your teacher, mother or dad that John Henry made you do it.

Let's examine this situation in more detail. The ruling says if someone walks into a tavern, gets drunk and kills somebody else, we can blame the tavern owners.

Is the next step to hold beer distributors and liquor stores responsible for drunken drivers and destructive party goers?

Will organizations, or even homeowners, be held liable because someone attended their party, got drunk, then went out and killed someone else?

What about someone who went to four or five taverns and had a couple drinks at each? Should only the last one be sued? The last two? Or maybe all of them?

Put yourself in the place of the bartenders in a busy tavern. How is that bartender to know who is driving and who are passengers? With a half-dozen people wanting drinks at the same time, should the bartender be expected to survey each before serving them?

We acknowledge that alcoholism and drunken driving are serious problems, and that sensible steps should be taken to reduce or eliminate abuses. But let's put the blame where it belongs – on the person consuming those drinks, not the one who's serving them.

Let's not allow money-grubbing attorneys to haul whomever they can into court just because the drunken driver or his estate has little or no money.

The Texas Supreme Court should admit it made a mistake and correct it as quickly as possible.

# # #

This last example was part of a three-editorials entry that won Utah's annual editorials writing contest – open to all media members in the state. The honor included a cash award of $100, which I received. The three editorials were published in *The Daily Herald* at Provo, Utah.

Why Not Wednesday Deer Opener?

Opening weekend of the Utah general deer season has made it clear Utah lawmakers need to do more than require all license holders to take the hunter safety course.

Opening weekend – and most particularly opening day – has become a chaotic circus at best, and a downright disaster to many who had hoped to enjoy a safe and sane outing, let alone take home some meat.

And with each year's opener, less sanity and less safety are apparent.

How can anyone enjoy a safe and sane deer hunt when hunters are spaced about every 75 to 100 yards?

How can anyone enjoy the camping experience when a hunter must drive to the end of a dead-end road on a ridge more than 9,000 feet high to find a secluded camping area?

Who enjoys camping bumper-to-bumper in RV cities?

Is it any wonder disheartened and discouraged hunters turn to road-hunting by the opening-day afternoon when the morning's insanity brings hunter orange too close for comfort from every direction?

One hunter, for example, reported it was "too dangerous" after bullets whined near him on opening day, sending him home later that day.

Some Uinta National Forest rangers call it "opening day mania." And add even they won't go hunting on the opening weekend.

A couple foresters remarked that it's gone so far that hunters can't even find a parking space along the main roads of the Uinta National Forests.

But what one forest supervisor finds so sad is that apparently almost no one cares – and that no one is trying to do anything about the situation.

So it's time for some of us to do something!

Big game management involves more than just promoting the greatest number of game animals for the available habitat. It also should involve managing hunting pressure.

Some ideas and possible alternatives:

- *The big game board could schedule a mid-week opener for the deer hunt – such as the one for the elk season, which opens on a Wednesday. Maybe that would reduce the opening-day mania.*

- *Limit deer licenses to every other year for each hunter.*

  State Division of Wildlife Resources workers won't like selling only half as many licenses each year unless they can charge twice as much. But anyone who is disgusted with the opening crowds should be agreeable to that.

- *Try splitting the deer season – like a couple other western states have done.*

Colorado and New Mexico did so, and forest workers noted pressure was reduced substantially on forest roads and facilities.

The foresters here have made the following suggestion: Have a three-day opener; then close the hunt for three days. Open again for a second season of five days; then close for another three days, and open a third time for a final season of seven days.

With that arrangement, hunters would be allowed to seek a permit for only one of the three seasons.

These suggestions are not the only options available, but it is evident that something should be done to reduce pressure and return safety to the deer hunt.

This editorial establishes somewhat of a challenge to lawmakers and wildlife managers. And it appeals to noble motives.

It cites sources, dramatizes ideas and strives to have readers agree with the statements and concepts it suggests.

The other two editorials in the award-winning entry cited the inability of Congress to collect billions of dollars in student load debts, and lauded a U.S. Supreme Court ruling that prevents the closure of certain criminal trials.

The student loans editorial included suggestions to prod repayment.

The award cited the "care and concern projected" by the editorials, and added they demonstrated that use of "the declarative sentence is not a lost art."

That same type of direct writing is what this entire book is designed to emphasize.

Ten Commandments of Good Writing

These 10 rules can help you write so people will understand you.

1. Keep Sentences Short.

   Use one thought per sentence.

2. Prefer the Simple to the Complex.

3. Avoid unnecessary words.

4. Prefer the Familiar Word.

   Use words that communicate your meaning.

5. Write as You Talk. –

   This is good advice for getting your message across.

   Vocalize your writing – under your breath, in a whisper, or even out loud. If it sounds easily understandable when you vocalize it, then maybe it will be quickly understood by readers.

   It may need a bit of polishing, but stick to this idea.

6. Use Terms Your Readers Can Picture.

7. Make Writing Relate to the Readers.

   Write to match their background and experience.

8. Write to Express – Not to Impress.

9. Put Action into Your Verbs.

   Passive tense fails to get results.

10. Make Full Use of Variety.

   Vary the length of sentences, paragraphs and style.
   Sometimes even slang is appropriate.

The Benefits of Writing

1. Writing can provide accuracy.
The accuracy of the spoken word declines as the message is passed from one person to the next. Any child who has played the game of gossip knows this is true.

2. Writing improves memory.
The average person loses 50 percent of what he or she hears immediately after hearing it.

Within 24 hours, the average person will forget another 25 percent. The mere act of taking notes improves retention.

3. Writing is precise and permanent.
Written messages allow us to maintain copies of our communications for use days, weeks, and years later.

Written communication s also allow us to share our knowledge, ideas and concepts with posterity.

4. Writing improves thinking.
Good writing requires logic and discipline

5. Writing improves speaking.
It's been proven: The more you improve your writing, the more your speaking improves.

6. Writing saves time.
It should be obvious that good writing – when clear and easy to read – will speed comprehension by those who need to understand the information.

7. Writing improves your image.
It provides the image of professionalism.

Most people will prefer your service if you look good on paper.

(Consider: Who would you prefer to perform your heart surgery? Would you prefer the intern with minimal experience; or the surgeon who has performed a half-dozen successful heart transplants?)

When Writing Articles and Reports

1. Grab the reader's attention with the beginning.

2. Come on strong.

Use active, convincing words and phrases.

Be positive, not negative.

3. Don't scare or intimidate the reader.

With too many pages

Or with long sentences and paragraphs

4. Ease into bad news.

5. Be discreet

You never know who might read what you have written.

And what you've written provides a record for reference

6. Be correct: With grammar, names, and titles.

7. Don't be lazy.

Use the thesaurus. Search for the best word.

Use the dictionary. Verify spellings and definitions.

8. Know the subject. Be sure of your "facts."

When in doubt, check and confirm.

Conclusions are open to debate. Facts are indisputable.

9. Avoid abbreviations and initials.

Don't make your reader search for the meaning of those initials.

10. Don't use etc., and avoid repeating favorite words.

11. Don't be flowery and pompous with inflated words.

Use only as many words as you need, and no more.

12. Be Clear.

13. Use words to suit your readers.

Use technical terms ONLY when ALL your readers – all -- know their meanings.

Otherwise, you must adequately EXPLAIN their meanings.

14. Be sure the reader knows who said what.

And the use of too many "he's" or "she's" can be confusing

15. Don't raise more questions than you answer.

16. Don't be cute.

17. Be modest.

18. Be neat.

19. End on a positive note.

20. Reread, edit and revise as often as necessary.

<u>Until you are proud of it</u>

A Description of Good Writers

1. Good Writers know the purpose of their writing before they start.
2. Good Writers proofread their work.
3. Good Writers edit and revise their work
4. Good Writers spend more time on their writing than do poor writers.

Essentials of a Good Newsletter

A good newsletter need be only one side of one page. But it may be necessary to provide a longer one as members and employees request or need additional information.

Longer newsletters are much more appreciated – particularly by members in those organizations that meet only once a month or less. But for organizations that meet frequently, more attention should be given to brevity of the items.

Membership readers don't like wading through long, flowery reports. Remember, the objective is to convey information quickly, accurately, with a touch of humor and, most importantly, in an easily readable manner.

Newsletters should **not** be considered as an opportunity for someone to impress the readers or express personal opinions.

Good Newsletters Provide:

■ *Recognition for those who perform well.*
Note the member or employee of the month
Cite awards and honors won by members

■ *Calendar of events.*
List any coming events – including those sponsored by other organizations – which may be of general interest to the membership.

■ *Reports on personnel changes.*
Report on new members or new employees
Include reports on promotions or new jobs
Give new address on someone who's leaving

■ *News of general interest.*
New policies and procedures – Most important
Births, deaths, birthdays and anniversaries
Tell changes coming soon, such as new equipment
Report accidents and member tragedies

■ *At least one humorous item per issue*

■ *But be sure it is news.*
Don't use an item 2 months old or so stale that
everyone already had knowledge of it 3 weeks ago.

Formal Speech Format

condensed from the book

Public Speaking as Listeners Like It
By Richard C. Borden – Copyright 1935

Ho Hum – *Light a Fire*

Your speech is not well organized unless you kindle a quick flame of spontaneous interest with your first sentence. (The same as with writing.)

Why Bring That Up? – *Build a Bridge*

Your listener lives on an island – an island of HIS interests.

You must <u>immediately</u> maintain the listener's attention by noting why this issue is important and how it affects the listener.

For Instance! – *Illustrate*

Listeners like for instances

- *In story form*
- *That involve famous people*
- *That animate the pages of history*
- *That are based on colorful analogies*
- *That are interwoven with visual aids*
- *That dramatize important statistics*

So What? – *Emphasize Your Point*

- *Ask for Action*
- *Tell What Is Needed*

Beauty and Life

(Originally published in *Stories from The Golden Throne*.)

I have kayaked the crystal clear lakes of New Hampshire and Montana;
Hiked the mountains of Utah, New Mexico and Pennsylvania;
Seen the beauty of desert flowers in Texas and California,
And looked down at my toes through chest-high salt water off the coast
of Florida.

I have seen the sea of sparkling left by ice storms,
Coating weeds and trees in Oklahoma and Missouri;
Watched sailing craft catching the wind
Off Rhode Island, Maine and Puerto Rico;
And driven past the sapphire red of rosebud trees
Lining the interstate through Virginia and Tennessee.

I've watched the dawn rise over the shores of New Jersey and
Maine;
Seen the sunsets from the peaks of Colorado and seaside hills of
Washington;
Driven through snowstorms in Wyoming and Arizona,
And experienced the electrifying lightning shows across the
night skies of western Kansas.

I've viewed Devil's Tower and the Grand Canyon;
Thrown snowballs in July in the Rockies;
Walked the edge of a mile-wide meteor crater;
Toured Yellowstone, Yosemite, the Smokies and the Everglades,
And snapped pictures of the bears and moose in Alaska.

I've seen whitetails slipping through the eastern hardwoods,
Enjoyed muleys feeding in mountain meadows;
Watched turkeys and elk sharing the same grove of aspens;
Chuckled at young raccoons devouring our camp scraps;
Rolled my eyes as a skunk came strolling under my lawn chair
near a dying campfire,
And smiled at mama porcupine and her kits as they sauntered
across the forest floor.

I've decided that tailored lawns and ruler-straight hedges of
Suburban wealth
Have nothing over the flaming orange and muted reds
Of an autumn mountainside in the Rockies,
Or the random multi-colors of October hillsides in the
Appalachians.

I've absorbed the values bestowed upon me by honest and
caring parents;
Learned to yearn for knowledge from the example of an older
brother;
Experienced the passion and love of several good women
With fewer faults and flaws than my own,
And too often suffered the grief of family deaths.

Of course, there is much I have not seen or experienced;
But I have doubts that what I have missed can outshine what I
already have done.
And through it all I have been blessed with good health and a
sharing with fine friends.
But the greatest blessing of all was being born in this great
country and into a good family.

So now I am savoring my retirement in Butte, Montana,
Where the pleasant disposition of the residents obviously is
affected
By the wealth of sunshine the city receives – especially all
winter;
And I will continue to enjoy as much more of this great life as my
modest means can provide.

By Darrell Berkheimer – August, 2008

The Golden Throne Story

CB's – Citizens Band radios – were quite popular back in the 1970s.

They still are widely used by truck drivers, and still might be in some areas of the nation.

I occasionally went on camping and hunting outings with a small group of outdoorsmen, and frequently took my family camping when I lived in Utah for many years. Our group had CB's in our RV's.

I also remember that I wanted a distinctive "handle" – as CB pseudonyms are called. I wanted a handle that no one else might use.

After my CB was installed in my pickup truck, I pondered different names for weeks. During that time, my family was going camping most weekends. And with a wife and daughters, we realized the need to acquire a porta-potty.

But when I priced them, I thought they were too expensive. So I decided to build one.

I bought a diaper pail with a lid. Then I made a box frame with scrap two-by-fours and plywood.

I took an old toilet seat and sawed a little off the sides and front to make it a bit square. Then I measured and mounted the toilet seat inside the box so that the seat would sit on top of the diaper pail lid and hold it in place when traveling.

I fashioned a lid for the box out of some more scrap plywood.

I bought a can of school-bus-yellow spray paint and sprayed the box. I acquired a scrap of gold velvet velour material and a piece of 3- to 4-inch thick foam rubber. I covered the top of the lid with the gold material over the foam rubber to provide a soft seat.

The result was a disguised porta-potty that had the appearance of a hassock.

It was dubbed "The Golden Throne."

So that became my distinctive CB handle.

Years later, when I was driving big trucks coast-to-coast, I started chatting on the CB with another truck driver as we were going through Kansas. He asked for my handle, and I said:

"I bet you never heard a handle like mine before. I'm The Golden Throne."

He surprised me when he said, "Yeah, I heard that handle once before."

"When and where was that?" I asked.

"Wait a minute, let me think," he said. Then he added, "Oh, I remember. It was last fall – last September – up in Wyoming. I overheard a couple fellows talking, and that's what the one guy called himself."

"That was me," I said.

Not long after that, I purchased a custom made,

silver-colored license plate.   On the right side is a gold toilet, inset on a red shield, with a dark blue sash diagonally across the shield.

It's my crest of arms.

In big gold letters on the left side of the license plate, it says "*The Golden Throne.*" And at the bottom of the plate is the word "Crusader" – in honor of my years spent writing newspaper columns and editorials.

I keep that license plate in the aluminum brief case that I used when driving coast-to-coast.

Now you know why I decided to name my first book "*Stories from The Golden Throne.*"

So this book has become another in *The Golden Throne* series.